IMAGES
of America

ELLENSBURG

IMAGES
of America

ELLENSBURG

Andrew Caveness and the
Ellensburg Public Library

ARCADIA
PUBLISHING

Published by Arcadia Publishing
Charleston, South Carolina

Library of Congress Control Number: 2009928853

For all general information contact Arcadia Publishing at:
Telephone 843-853-2070
Fax 843-853-0044
E-mail sales@arcadiapublishing.com
For customer service and orders:
Toll-Free 1-888-313-2665

Visit us on the Internet at www.arcadiapublishing.com

*This book is dedicated to Melissa, Nicole, and Eliza:
three ladies who give me strength, hope, and fulfillment.*

CONTENTS

ACKNOWLEDGMENTS

I would like to thank the wonderful and helpful staff of the Ellensburg Public Library. Director Debby DeSoer was enthusiastic about the project from day one and was instrumental in getting it off the ground. Milton Wagy, the local history librarian extraordinaire, is of a rare breed: dedicated, knowledgeable, tireless, enthusiastic, and, above all, motivating. Milton has amassed a wealth of knowledge about Ellensburg, and his countless suggestions and corrections were invaluable to me. I can't thank him enough.

And to Arcadia Publishing, who made this entire process much smoother than I had expected. If only all editors could be like Sarah Higginbotham! She was supportive, encouraging, helpful, and always there if I needed anything.

Finally, I would like to thank my wonderful family. Melissa, Nicole, and Eliza: words cannot express what you mean to me. This book is your book; your understanding when daddy was gone researching and your interest in looking at what pictures I had discovered made it all worthwhile. I love you!

Ellensburg was initially spelled "Ellensburgh," but in 1894, the "H" was dropped by the U.S. Post Office. To avoid confusion, the author only uses the current spelling.

Unless otherwise noted, all pictures are courtesy of the Ellensburg Public Library.

INTRODUCTION

One of the earliest recorded descriptions of Ellensburg's setting was from Alexander Ross, an employee with the North West Fur Company, who came to the Kittitas Valley in 1814 looking to purchase horses from the Kittitas Indians. The valley was home to the Kittitas band of the Yakama Indians, yet every year in the spring and fall, Native Americans from all over the region converged on Che-lo-han, a massive rendezvous to trade, gamble, hunt, gather camas root, and congregate. When Ross came from Fort Okanogan seeking horses, he was in awe of the campsite. "We could see the beginning but not the end! It was a grand and imposing sight in the wilderness, covering more than six miles in every direction." The reason the Kittitas Valley was chosen for the gathering is the same reason white settlers embraced it so enthusiastically 50 years later: location. The Kittitas Valley is at a natural crossroads in eastern Washington, and its fertile lowland was excellent grazing ground.

Less than 50 years after Alexander Ross came to trade for horses, a young cowboy named Andrew Jackson "A. J." Splawn was hired to drive cattle from the Yakima Valley to the Cariboo mines in British Columbia, Canada. Splawn, along with other cowboys, headed north and reached the Kittitas Valley toward the end of August 1861. Splawn later recounted his first glimpse of the Kittitas Valley, "This valley, as it looked to me that day, was the loveliest spot I had ever seen . . . it was truly a land of plenty." Splawn and the others, in awe of the scenery, knew that it would not be long before the settlers would discover "this Eden." The Kittitas Valley was an important location for the cattle drivers because it not only offered ample grazing grass and fresh water, but its locale allowed the cowboys to set up camp near present-day downtown Ellensburg and be able to see the cattle for miles in every direction.

As a result of the intermingling of cowboy cattle drivers and Native Americans, a trade began to flourish. While it could have been a hostile situation, it was more the opposite. The Native Americans knew the cowboys were there temporarily, and they had items to barter. Yet the natives of the valley were wary, warning the cowboys of the harsh, cold winters, hoping to dissuade them from seeking more permanent settlements. But it was not long before settlers fell in love with the valley too, and white settlement was all but inevitable.

In the late 1850s to early 1860s, things began to change. First, the Yakima War, which lasted until 1858, resulted in an increased military presence in the Kittitas and Yakima Valleys, as well as most of the Native Americans being chased out of the Kittitas Valley and onto the newly established reservation in Yakima. Second, the influx of settlers, cowboys, prospectors, and military men in and around the Kittitas Valley led to the discovery of the cherished land that only a handful of white people had ever seen. Several temporary cowboy camps became more permanent, and by the end of the 1860s, the Kittitas Valley would see its first permanent white settlers.

After failed attempts, settlement in the present-day Ellensburg was finally successful in 1867. Frederick Ludi, a Swiss immigrant, was working the Montana mines and had saved enough money to head to the Puget Sound area to find a permanent home. Ludi, along with his coworker

"Dutch" John Galler, were traveling to the Seattle area when they came upon the Kittitas Valley. Ludi, like those before him, was at a loss for words when he viewed the valley for the first time and vowed to go no farther. He and Galler settled just south of present-day downtown Ellensburg in 1868. This cabin became the first permanent white home in Ellensburg. Ludi kept true to his word, for he never left Ellensburg, and his original farm became part of Ellensburg in 1882 when he gave his land to the city.

The next permanent settler was Tillman Houser, who came in the spring of 1868 from Renton, Washington, and built a cabin northeast of Ellensburg. Houser raised sheep on his farm, and during the winter of 1868, there were three settlements in the area. The next few years, however, the valley saw a huge influx of settlers as more people sought land east of the Cascade Mountains. The trail leading from the Puget Sound to the Kittitas Valley had been improved, which facilitated settlers heading east and cattle drivers heading west to the new market. Around this time, cowboys began driving cattle into the Kittitas Valley to graze for the summer, then over Snoqualmie Pass to the Puget Sound area to be sold for a premium. This new "road" secured Ellensburg's success.

Cattle drivers entering the valley, along with the new settlements popping up seemingly overnight, created a demand for business. A. J. Splawn, pasturing his cattle in the valley in 1870, decided to start a store with Ben Burch, another cowboy camped in the area. Splawn bought a small cabin from William "Bud" Wilson and had it moved near their camp, which was in the heart of the present downtown area. On November 20, 1870, Splawn arrived with goods received at The Dalles, Oregon, and stocked the store full of the newly acquired merchandise. In good spirit, a young settler John Gillespie named the store Robber's Roost, which took Splawn by surprise but was kept. Soon the store became popular with settlers, cowboys, and Native Americans.

In 1871, Seattleites wanted to build a wagon road from Seattle to the Kittitas Valley, which would require immense improvements of the trail that led over Snoqualmie Pass. John Alden Shoudy, who was working in Seattle for his brother-in-law, Dexter Horton, represented Seattle in this endeavor. Shoudy crossed the Cascades and entered the Kittitas Valley in the summer of 1871. Once reaching present-day Ellensburg, Shoudy decided to purchase the Robber's Roost from Splawn, who was interested in getting out of the retail business and returning to the cattle business. In the spring of 1872, Shoudy decided that this new location would become his permanent home. He built a second log cabin near his store and sent for his family, who had remained in Seattle waiting until he established a home. Shoudy's family arrived safely, and the store's business began to grow daily with the new arrivals to the valley.

When Shoudy took over the Robber's Roost from Splawn, he also received Splawn's 160 acres of land, originally acquired via squatter's rights. The land Shoudy received is the present-day downtown portion of Ellensburg. In 1873, Shoudy had his land surveyed by A. L. Knowlton, and he began to devise the early plans for a town. Yet the area was still isolated, and fear of Native Americans led the early settlers to build a stockade on Shoudy's land that was to serve as a secure fortress. The stockade was laid out in Shoudy's plat for the city, encompassing the block now occupied by the Davidson building, yet it was never needed.

The auditor of Yakima County recorded Shoudy's plat for the new city—named Ellen's Burgh after his wife, Mary Ellen Shoudy—on April 10, 1875. At the time, Ellensburg was still part of Yakima County, and Washington was still a territory, so Shoudy had to travel to Yakima to file his plat for Ellensburg. Shoudy sold the town lots for $2 per residence and $10 per businesses, and the town began to grow immediately. Shoudy kept the lots on the northwest corner of Third Avenue and Main Street and, in 1876, built the first frame building in the valley. This building was a large, two-story structure that served as an improved store and meeting hall on the second floor.

What started as a small store had become a growing city within five years, and Ellensburg showed great promise. Shoudy's frame building on Main Street was replaced by a brick structure, and many of the buildings in town were of brick and stone construction, which attests to the growing capital of the city and the wealth of the new citizens. By the mid-1880s, Ellensburg was growing rapidly, surpassing the city of North Yakima and on its way to becoming the county seat of Yakima County. Yet many of the residents of Ellensburg felt that the Kittitas Valley should break away from Yakima County and form its own county. Shoudy was elected the Yakima County representative for the Washington territorial legislature in 1882, and he quickly began to push a bill creating Kittitas County. Shoudy's bill was successful, and Kittitas County separated from Yakima County in 1883. On November 26, 1883, Ellensburg was officially incorporated as a city in the two-day-old Kittitas County.

In 1887, only 16 years after Shoudy arrived in the valley, there were 195 houses, 45 barns, 3 livery stables, 1 feed stable, 3 hotels, 5 restaurants, 3 lodging houses, 12 saloons, and many more stores, schools, and businesses in Ellensburg. The city also received a railroad line, the Northern Pacific Railway, in 1886. In fact, Ellensburg was growing so rapidly and had so much promise that when Washington Territory became a state in 1889, Ellensburg was one of the top three cities selected for the state capital. Olympia, Ellensburg, and North Yakima were the three choices for state capital, and many felt Ellensburg was the best choice due to its centrality in the state and the promise the city held.

Hopes for the capital were dashed on July 4, 1889, when a fire destroyed the entire downtown district in a matter of hours. The fire began in J. S. Anthony's grocery store on Main Street between Fourth and Fifth Avenues, and the notably strong wind in Ellensburg carried the flames through the buildings, including ones of brick and stone, with such speed and force that the meager fire department and their hand-pulled hose reels were no match for the blaze. The cause of the fire is unknown, but the result was all too clear. The town lost all its saloons, most of the lodging houses, most of the businesses, and many residences. Before the ashes cooled, business owners in town were planning to rebuild the city, but soon after, Olympia was selected as the capital of Washington state. Ellensburg was, however, selected as the location for the State Normal School, or teacher college. The people of Ellensburg rebuilt the city, and the brick buildings constructed to replace those burned are still there today. Many have had a face-lift, and many more have been remodeled, but the skeleton of the buildings remains the same.

In 1891, the Washington State Normal School began in Ellensburg. Since it lacked its own building, classes were held on the second floor of the large Washington School. Beginning with four faculty members and about 50 students, the normal school began small but quickly grew. Construction began on a building for the school, and Barge Hall, named for the first school president, opened in 1894.

After the Panic of 1893, which financially affected most of the country, including Ellensburg business owners, much of the progress in Ellensburg was halted, and many businesses continued failing. Yet, by 1897, the worst was over, and Ellensburg renewed its vigorous growth into the 20th century. One major key to Ellensburg's growth was the completion of irrigation canals that made it possible to convert desert sagebrush land into prime farming land. Irrigation work began as early as the 1870s, and by the early part of the 20th century, more than half the valley was irrigated and land was used for farming. The new source of water provided the valley with the opportunity to grow corn, fruit, grains, and hay on a large scale. Hay became the No. 1 crop, and much of it was shipped out of the valley on the Northern Pacific Railway as early as the 1880s. The export of hay was, and still is, profitable, and allowed Ellensburg to thrive.

In 1909, the Chicago, Milwaukee, and Saint Paul Railroad line was put through Ellensburg, giving the town two railroads and facilitating travel between Ellensburg and Seattle to the west and Ellensburg and Chicago to the east. This brought more people to town and provided another means of import and export to the valley.

In the 1920s, wanting to pay homage to the cowboy legacy of the valley, locals gathered and planned to construct rodeo grounds at the foot of Craig's Hill. In the spring of 1923, hundreds of volunteers within a 15-mile radius of town showed up and converted the vacant land into a fine rodeo ground, seemingly overnight. By the fall of 1923, the Ellensburg Rodeo had begun, which is still a major event and the No. 1 attractant in the valley today.

World War II brought an influx of men to Ellensburg as the college became a training center for pilots, using the airport north of town. The army selected Ellensburg as the location for the training center for the 314th detachment, which stimulated the economy and expanded the newly named Bowers Field and the original airport. After the war, the college saw a boom in enrollment as veterans sought to use the Servicemen's Readjustment Act of 1944, or the G. I. Bill, for higher education. The college has maintained a steady growth to this day.

Ellensburg has seen many changes since it began as a small trading post, yet it has retained a firm grip on its heritage. Many of the historic downtown buildings have been restored to their original appearances, placards have been added to denote historically significant locations and buildings around town, and there are many citizens intent on revitalizing the downtown area and preserving the rich history Ellensburg has to share.

One
BEGINNINGS

A picture of tepees on a creek in the Kittitas Valley, taken in the 1890s, shows the type of tepee used by the Kittitas Indians, how close they lived to water, and the arrangement of their homes. The Kittitas Valley has many winding streams, and the Native Americans lived along them, as did the settlers who came in the 1860s and 1870s.

A view of Che-lo-han, which were big trade and council grounds where the Kittitas Indians played host to several other tribes from the region. Che-lo-han was situated about 10 miles northeast of downtown Ellensburg and was located there because of the centrality of the Kittitas Valley in the region. In 1814, Alexander Ross, working for the North West Fur Company, noted that the camp covered 6 miles and was a grand site. A. J. Splawn also commented on the immense size of the encampment when he rode through the valley in the 1860s. In the 1890s, when this picture was taken, there were still a number of Native Americans who came and camped here, though it is private land today. It is rumored that the original racetrack used by the Native Americans can still be seen today, permanently etched into the valley floor.

Uu-hi.

Chief Owhi was the principle chief of the Kittitas band of the Yakama Indians in the mid-19th century. Owhi was Yakama chief Kamiakin's uncle and Qualchan's father. Kamola Hall, on Central Washington University's campus, was named after Owhi's daughter. Owhi signed the Yakima Treaty of 1855 with territorial governor Isaac I. Stevens in Walla Walla, but a few years later, he was accused of killing settlers and leading resistance against the U.S. Army. In 1858, Owhi was captured by Col. George Wright near present-day Spokane and was used as bait to capture his son, Qualchan. Qualchan entered the camp and was immediately hung. Owhi later attempted to escape but was shot from his horse and died two hours later. Owhi's nephew, Kamiakin, fled to Canada but returned after things calmed down. He died in 1877 near Rock Lake in the Washington Territory.

Born in North Carolina in 1835, Ben Snipes's family later moved to Iowa, where he was schooled. In 1852, at the age of 17, he struck out on his own. In 1858, Snipes purchased cattle and began driving his own herd in the Yakima Valley. In 1860, he drove his cattle to the Okanogan mining district and sold all his cattle, making good money. He eventually bought land in Yakima and began raising cattle on his estimated 6,000 acres. By 1880, Snipes owned about 35,000 head of cattle and a great number of horses. In 1886, Snipes entered into the banking business in Ellensburg and then opened a bank in Roslyn in 1890. After a robbery in Roslyn and the Panic of 1893, Snipes left the area and moved to Seattle. He died in 1906 at age 71 in his home in Seattle.

Andrew Jackson Splawn was born in Missouri in 1845 and moved to Oregon in 1851. In 1861, he relocated to Yakima County in the Washington Territory to live with his older brother, Charles, and entered the cattle business. In 1870, Splawn and his friend Ben Burch bought a cabin to begin a trading post in the Kittitas Valley. John Gillispie, a young settler, offered to make a sign for the store and called it Robber's Roost. Splawn sold this store to John A. Shoudy in 1871 and returned to the cattle business. Later Splawn became involved in the Washington State Legislature in 1902 as a state senator. He was the first mayor of North Yakima from 1911 to 1914 as well. In 1915, Splawn went to the Pan-American Exposition in San Francisco as the live stock commissioner from the state of Washington. Splawn died on March 2, 1917, at his home in North Yakima.

This is another view of Che-lo-han, the great Native American encampment held near Ellensburg. Chief Moses, from the area now encompassed by Moses Lake, Washington, used to visit the camp every year. Chief Moses helped save A. J. Spawn's life when Splawn was passing through in the 1860s and offered protection to town founder John A. Shoudy during hostile encounters between new settlers and Native Americans. There was a racetrack on the bluff behind the rock outcropping where Native Americans would put their horses to the test and wager against one another.

Born in Switzerland in 1833, Frederick Ludi came to America at age 19 to work with his brother. He then worked the mines in Montana until 1867, when his friends' advice enticed him to head west. He and "Dutch" John Galler, a coworker, headed for Puget Sound to seek permanent homes. When they reached the Kittitas Valley in August 1867, Ludi was so entranced by the scenery that he claimed he would never live anywhere else. He and Galler moved to the east side of the Yakima River in 1868 and began a farm in what is now southern Ellensburg. Not long after, Galler moved away, but Ludi never left. In 1882, Ludi retired, sold his farm—which later became platted into city property—and moved in with Carl A. Sander. Frederick Ludi died in 1916 at Sander's home and is buried in the International Order of Odd Fellows (IOOF) cemetery. Ludi was the first permanent white residence in the Kittitas Valley, and he is credited with naming Wilson Creek.

Tillman Houser was born in Pennsylvania on March 31, 1840, and was a farmer until he enlisted in the Civil War in 1862. Later Houser moved west and lived for two and a half years on Puget Sound, then moved to Renton, Washington, and spent a year and a half there, until the fall of 1868. In 1868, he came to Kittitas Valley with his family in search of farmland to raise sheep. Houser, his wife, Louise Werkhiser Houser, and their three children, Sarah, Harrison, and Clarence, moved to the Kittitas Valley, staking a claim 12 miles northeast of Ellensburg near present-day Schnebly road. It took them 15 days to travel from Seattle to the Kittitas Valley over the Cascade Mountains, and Houser had to cut a road for 3 miles. The Houser family was the first white family to call the Kittitas Valley home. After settling in the valley, the Housers had three more children, Pernina, Alva, and Amelia. Houser died in 1918 at his home in Ellensburg.

John Alden Shoudy was born in Illinois in 1842 and worked his father's farm to put himself through business school. After school, he enlisted for the Civil War and served three years. After the war, he moved to California to live with his brother-in-law Dexter Horton, where he met and married Mary Ellen Stewart. They moved to Seattle in 1868, but in 1871, Shoudy came to the Kittitas Valley as a representative of Seattle business owners who wanted to build a road from Seattle to the Kittitas Valley over the Cascade Mountains. Shoudy bought Splawn's store and moved his family over from Seattle to the Kittitas Valley. In 1875, he platted a town and sold plots to settlers and businesspersons, naming the town Ellensburg for his wife, Mary Ellen. He was a member of the Territorial Legislature in 1883, and he was instrumental in the formation of Kittitas County. He was also a member of the state Constitutional Convention in 1889 and tried to have Ellensburg named the state capital. Shoudy died unexpectedly at his home in Ellensburg on May 25, 1901.

Mary Ellen Stewart was born in 1846 in Kentucky and crossed the California Plains as a child with her family. They settled in Oakland, California, where she met and married John Alden Shoudy in 1867. Mary Ellen was a quiet lady and not very involved in Ellensburg society. She moved to Seattle later in life and died in 1921.

This is an artist's depiction of Robber's Roost, the trading post that John Shoudy purchased from A. J. Splawn in 1871. This small trading post was located in the center of the Kittitas Valley on Wilson Creek. A. J. Splawn and Ben Burch began this store, which was the location of their summer camp during cattle pasturage in the valley. The future city of Ellensburg would grow outward from this historic location.

20

Robber's Roost was a success, so John A. Shoudy expanded it into a new building on the present corner of Third Avenue and Main Street. This store was much larger than the previous and was located close to the original location. Capitalizing on his success, Shoudy replaced this store with a large brick building on the same location, but it burned in the fire of 1889.

John and Mary Ellen Shoudy (on the porch behind the barrel) stand in front of their Family Store on Main Street, which had come a long way since the original Robber's Roost. This picture was taken around 1885 and shows the prominent couple among other locals in the town they started.

Taken in Seattle, Ellensburg town founder John A. Shoudy (left) poses with his brother William. William came west with his sister, Hannah Eliza Horton, and her husband, Dexter Horton, in 1852 via the Oregon Trail. William lived his life in Seattle, was a prominent businessman, and served as mayor in 1886. John A. Shoudy was a business partner with Dexter Horton before he came to the Kittitas Valley.

This early view of the southeast corner of Third Avenue and Main Street shows the New Corner, which was was near Shoudy's original Robber's Roost. The New Corner boasted a bar, a barbershop, hot or cold baths, and a hot meal. On the left is the Gem Restaurant, and just past that was a shooting gallery where patrons could try out their marksmanship. This building was destroyed by one of the early fires in Ellensburg.

The Shoudy residence, pictured here, was located just north of Fifth Avenue on the west side of Water Street. This photograph, taken in 1885, shows the young Shoudy family posed in front of their home. They are, from left to right, John Jr., Loyola, Lilly, Etta, Laura, Chester, John A. Shoudy, and Mary Ellen peeking out the window. The right half of this house still stands, roughly in the same location, and serves as apartments.

Ben Snipes built this beautiful stone building for his new bank at the southeast corner of Fourth Avenue and Pearl Street in 1887–1888. Pictured here is the first horse show in Ellensburg during the late fall of 1888 or the early spring of 1889. Charles Helm, a local horse rancher, owned the center horse, which sold for $1,200.

The Rehmke Brothers Gallery was on the north side of Fourth Avenue between Main and Pearl Streets. The Rehmke brothers were born in Germany in the 1850s but immigrated to the United States and arrived in Ellensburg in 1883. They first established a jewelry shop, but by 1885, they had converted it into a photography shop. This picture, taken in 1885, includes, from left to right, ? Privett; ? Bandy; Charlie Nason; Frank Simpson; Henry Rehmke, hidden behind the mule's head; ? Stoud; and Rehmke's brother William, in the door. Nason was born about 1830 in the Kittitas Valley. He was friendly to the early white settlers and helped them maintain peaceable relationships with other Native Americans in the valley. This building was close to where the fire of 1889 began, and it was completely destroyed in seconds. The Rehmkes built a new two-story, brick building in its place after the fire, and the building today houses a popular local bar.

The newly constructed Kittitas County Courthouse, which was located in the same spot as the current courthouse, is visible above. Kittitas County officially separated from Yakima County in 1883, and work began to construct a new courthouse, which was completed in 1887. John A. Shoudy's 1875 plan for Ellensburg designated an entire block, from Fifth to Sixth Avenues and from Main to Water Streets, as the courthouse block. This courthouse also had a jail in the north end of the building and housed the sheriff's office and a courtroom. It was called courthouse square because of the nicely landscaped grounds, which had a sweeping lawn and ample shade trees around the perimeter. In the 1950s, this building was deemed unsafe, and work began on a new courthouse that still serves the county today. Kittitas County sheriff Levy V. Winegar (Wynegar) is pictured wearing a derby hat and standing fourth from the right. Winegar married John A. Shoudy's niece, Carrie Shoudy.

Thomas Johnson built the Johnson House Hotel in 1884 at the northwest corner of Fourth Avenue and Pearl Street. The third floor was a ballroom; the lower two were the hotel proper. The huge frame structure was destroyed by the 1889 fire. Johnson, an early pioneer, operated the first stage line from Ellensburg to The Dalles, Oregon. The Ellensburg Masons met here before constructing their own building.

This building, on the corner of Fourth Avenue and Main Street, exemplifies a typical saloon and lodging house in the 1880s in Ellensburg. The first floor was a bar, as can be ascertained by the wood slats covering the windows to hide the debauchery inside. On the second floor were rooms to rent and likely a hot bath.

The Lynch Block, on the southwest corner of Fifth Avenue and Pearl Street, was built by Patrick Lynch in 1888 for $20,000. The structure was one of the few downtown buildings that survived the fire of 1889. The Johnson Hotel temporarily leased the upper portion of this building after the fire, offering 20 rooms to rent.

Constructed in 1882, this building was on the north side of Main Street between Third and Fourth Avenues, and represents what much of downtown Ellensburg looked like before the fire of 1889. The first floor contained a saloon, as apparent by the coverings on the windows. Early Ellensburg had many saloons downtown, which served as a means to share news, congregate, and consume liquor.

Ellensburg men gather on the porch of the *Kittitas Standard* newspaper office in 1884. Standing from left to right are Elmer Lockwood, Sam Packwood, five unidentified men, town founder John A. Shoudy (crooked derby hat and bow tie), Dr. Middleton Amen, Joseph LeClerc, John H. Stevens, Jeremiah Damman, and Arthur Damman. Sitting is John Burmeister, a German saloon keeper in town.

This *c.* 1885 picture was taken on the north side of Main Street between Third and Fourth Avenues. Dr. Thomas J. Newland and Dr. Isaac N. Power shared an office on the first floor, and prominent citizen Austin Mires had his law office on the second floor. As can be seen by the pole, there was a barbershop on the right.

This is a view looking north up the tracks toward the Northern Pacific Railway depot in Ellensburg in 1894. A key part to Ellensburg's early success was when the Northern Pacific Railway decided to run its line through town. John A. Shoudy donated much of the land to secure the train and a depot, and the first train arrived in March 1886. This depot served for many years until 1909, when the current one was built.

An early view of Ellensburg, taken in 1886, shows how small the budding town was. The large white building on the right was the Ellensburg Academy, a school that later became the First Presbyterian Church of Ellensburg. The building with three stories in the center is the Johnson House Hotel. Nearly every building in this picture was destroyed by a massive fire in 1889.

The McGrath and Palmer Livery Stables, located on the corner of Fifth Avenue and Main Street, are shown here in a picture taken around 1887. Clarence Palmer bought out his half and became sole owner later on. This location changed with the times and became an auto taxi shop later. This building survived the fire since it was northwest of the blaze.

This secondhand store was located just south of the not-yet-built Ben Snipes Bank on Pearl Street. The foundation for Snipes's bank can be seen at the lower left, which was completed before the fire of 1889. Harry M. Bryant and Edwin A. Willis were co-owners of the store. It was destroyed in the fire of 1889.

Two

INDEPENDENCE DAY
FIRE OF 1889

The 1893 Ellensburg Fire Department hose team No. 1 stands in front of the station at city hall on Pine Street between Third and Fourth Avenues. In the event of a fire, the hose cart was hand-pulled by the men to the fire. This station was home to the fire department after the fire of 1889 until 1910, when it was moved to a new station on Fourth Avenue

This view looking south on Pearl Street from Fifth Avenue was drawn for *Northwest Magazine* in April 1889, three months before the fire. On the right is the newly finished Lynch Block, which survived the fire. Nearly every other building in the picture was completely destroyed in the flames. The fire station, which had a hose cart, a hand pump, and a bell to summon help from volunteers, is the small wooden building at right with the open door. The Johnson House Hotel, in the distance on the right with smoke rising from a chimney, was where the Knights of Pythias held a dance on the Fourth of July, the night of the fire. Partygoers were the first to notice the flames, which started down the alley to the west, and everyone managed to exit the building just before it caught fire. This picture represents early Ellensburg at its pinnacle, when it was in contention to be the state capital, business flourished, the railroad brought a new source of wealth, and spirits were high.

This photograph shows the town as it looked after the fire of July 4, 1889, which decimated Ellensburg. The fire began at 10:30 p.m., and by 3:30 a.m. it had run its course and was out of fuel. The fire started in J. S. Anthony's grocery store on Main Street, yet the cause of the blaze is still unclear. Many speculated that it was arson, and some have wondered if errant fireworks were to blame, but there is no definitive cause. This view, looking north on Pearl Street from about Second Avenue, shows the complete devastation. The stone building on the right is the Ben Snipes Bank, where only a few exterior walls remain. On the far right, a building still smolders, and beyond that are the remains of the Masonic Temple. At the end of Pearl Street, on the left, is the intact Lynch Block building, which managed to escape the flames. Miraculously, no one died in the fire.

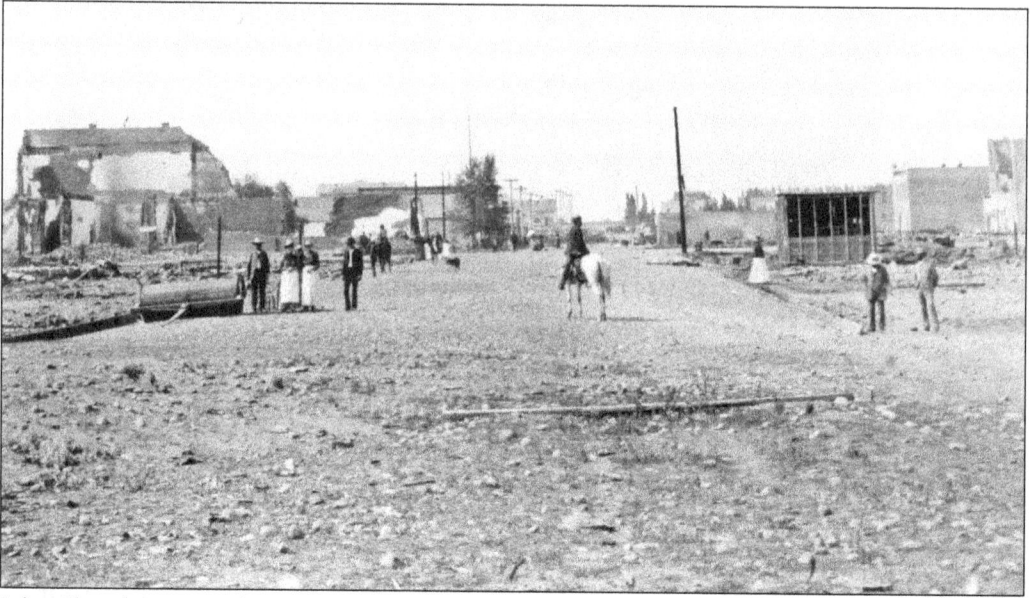

John Shoudy's original corner, which housed the first frame building in Ellensburg, is on the extreme left, reduced to rubble. Looking north, the fire began on the right side of the street, across from the large tree, but jumped Main Street and burned down both sides. The roof of the courthouse can be seen to the left of the tree, which was upwind from the fire and thus avoided being burned.

The fire blazed across Third Avenue, as seen in this view looking east from Water Street. The remains of Shoudy's building are on the left where the sidewalk led before it burned in the fire. Many of the buildings that burned south of Third Avenue were residences, and the fire occurred when many people were sleeping, but the commotion and sounds from the fire provided enough time for the people to escape.

The newly constructed Ellensburg Masonic Temple, which sat on the northwest corner of Fourth Avenue and Pine Street, is shown here as it looked in 1888. The temple held its first meeting in the building in February 1889, only five months before it would be completely destroyed by fire. The Masons relocated, but the corner of the building remained and is still there today.

The Masonic Temple stood two blocks east of where the fire began and was burnt completely. Some quick-thinking members managed to grab the minutes book and possibly a few other items before it burned, which are still in possession of the Ellensburg Masons. The Masons met at various locations until they moved into a new temple on Sixth Avenue in 1890, which they still use to this day.

The southern edge of the fire's wrath was the street in the foreground, Second Avenue. Shoudy's house is in the distance in the middle of the photograph, which remained untouched by the flames yet sat as a silent witness to the destruction. The empty land between the photographer and the buildings was mostly houses, all destroyed except a fortunate outhouse.

The ornate, stone Snipes Bank building is shown as it appeared on the morning of July 5, 1889. The stones withstood the intense heat, but the interior was entirely wood-framed; therefore, the building was gutted. The walls were temporarily held up but were not salvageable. Snipes rebuilt another bank at the same location with many of the same stones.

The people of Ellensburg met a few days after the fire and decided to begin rebuilding as soon as possible. Seemingly overnight, what were ashes and ruins was a flurry of construction and rebuilding. On the right is the Cadwell Building, which now houses the Kittitas County Historical Museum, and on the left is the Lloyd Opera House, which remained until the building was demolished in the 1950s.

Construction is everywhere as Ellensburg is rebuilt, as evident by the work on Pearl Street. Looking north from Third Avenue, seemingly every building is in various stages of construction. The pile of lumber sits in the middle of Pearl Street as the entire downtown district was put on hold while the rebuilding occurred.

Another view of Ellensburg's rebirth is pictured here, only a few weeks after the fire. The pile of stones was for the Snipes Bank, many of which were recycled from the first building. The building in the center, once the location of the Johnson House Hotel, is the Cadwell-Olympic Block building, which housed the popular Warwick Saloon on the first floor after it was reconstructed.

The fire department's new home was on the north side of Fourth Avenue, between Water and Kittitas Streets. The old location on Pine Street did not allow enough room for the equipment and horses, so the department relocated to a larger facility. Completed in 1910, the fire department used this station until the 1950s, when it was moved to its current location on Pearl Street.

Joseph W. Shull is sitting on the new steam fire engine purchased after the fire of 1889. The two white horses, Star and Jim, were the prize steeds of the Ellensburg Fire Department. When the alarm would sound, the two horses would walk under their harnesses and wait, knowing their duties and reflecting the great discipline they had.

The Kreidel Building, constructed during the fall and winter of 1889 by Samuel Kreidel, was an impressive Ellensburg landmark. Located on the northeast corner of Third Avenue and Pearl Street, the building was modernized during the 1940s with the removal of the familiar tower and ornate facade. In this picture, workers are putting the finishing touches on the cupola. The cover of this book showcases the Kreidel Building in its prime.

Washington National Bank, ELLENSBURG, Wash.

After the fire, Ben E. Snipes rebuilt his stone bank on the southeast corner of Fourth Avenue and Pearl Street. This building was just as massive and ornate as the first one, and had office space to rent on the side. After a few good years, Snipes had some setbacks that forced him to close this bank. First, his other bank in Roslyn, Washington, was robbed, and Snipes lost a large amount of money. Second, the Panic of 1893 was a major financial downfall that affected many people in Ellensburg, including Snipes. The building sat in limbo for a few years until it was purchased in 1906 and renamed the Washington National Bank. After World War II, the building received a major face-lift, and the stone exterior was removed and replaced with modern plaster and marble. There were two additions to the building, one in 1963 and the other in 1970, and the name changed again. Currently, the building is a Wells Fargo bank, doing business in the same "skeleton" that was built on the ashes of the first bank in 1889.

This building is by far the most photographed and iconic structure in downtown Ellensburg today. Designed by J. B. Randal and built by John B. Davidson, an Ellensburg attorney, the building cost $42,000 to construct in 1889. The two-story, 90-by-120-foot building was constructed of brick shipped from Chicago. Completed in January 1890, a large phoenix statue was placed on the Fourth Avenue side, and it has often been called the Phoenix Block since then. The phoenix was a mythical bird that rose anew from the ashes, much the way Ellensburg did, hence the usage on the Davidson Building. Businesses have always occupied the ground floor, and various hotels have been located in the second story. The Albany Hotel occupied the second floor in this photograph, which offered a great view of downtown, especially the corner room, which was always in demand and was the most expensive.

The Hotel Horton was located on the southwest corner of Sixth and Pearl Streets. The large two-story hotel was completed in 1890, contained 95 steam-heated rooms, and claimed to be one of the most comfortable and accommodating businesses in the Northwest. The structure was built by two Kansans, John Moffett and W. M. Dignon. The cost of the structure was $55,000, and the citizens of Ellensburg contributed $5,000 of the cost to show their support. The promoters advertised the new structure as being heated by steam and lighted by electricity. The hotel was in the final stages of construction when the July 4, 1889, fire swept through the city, leaving the "new palace" unscathed. The hotel was officially completed in 1890. The Hotel Horton was later named the Antlers Hotel and was completely destroyed by fire in October 1967.

Three

BUSINESS AND GROWTH

This photograph looks north on Pearl Street from Third Avenue. On the right is the Kreidel Building, and in the distance on the right is the Davidson Building. This pre-automobile picture shows how a mixture of bicycles, horses, and pedestrians shared the street. The tall building on the left is the Kleinberg Building, the only three-story brick building remaining in Ellensburg. Just beyond the Kleinberg is the Boss Bakery, which housed the Gilmour Grocery on the first floor.

JOHN A. SHOUDY
FOUNDER OF ELLENSBURGH.

R. P. 7

MILL PROPERTY OF SHOUDY & TJOSSEM.
ELLENSBURGH WASH. TER.

The City Mills was located near the Northern Pacific train depot in Ellensburg and was owned by John A. Shoudy and Rasmus P. Tjossem. A branch of Wilson Creek was diverted into a flume, where the waterpower generated electricity for the mill. In the larger picture of the mill, the original train depot can be seen on the right, and the Johnson House Hotel can be seen on the far left. The inset picture shows how the creek was used to generate the power, spinning a turbine before continuing on its path. Tjossem had a gristmill 4 miles south of Ellensburg in 1879 but partnered with Shoudy for the City Mills in 1885. The partnership dissolved a year later, with the two men running their own mills. Shoudy and his son, Dexter, ran the City Mills, while Tjossem and his son, Albert, built a new mill a couple of miles south of town. Both mills ran into the 20th century.

The Tjossem and Son flour mill is shown here about 3 miles south of downtown Ellensburg. This mill was built in 1889 by R. P. Tjossem after he split from the City Mills. The Tjossem Pond, as it was called then, was made by Tjossem, but it provided much entertainment to people year-round. In the summer, people swam in the pond, and in the winter, they ice-skated on it. The pond also provided income when, during the winter months, the ice was cut into blocks and stored in one of the two huge icehouses erected near a spur of the Northern Pacific rail line. The ice was then shipped via train to cities on the West Coast to be used in iceboxes. The mill burned in 1943, and a long-standing legacy came to an end.

The Electric Light and Power Plant, located on the Yakima River northwest of Ellensburg, harnessed the power of the Yakima River, making Ellensburg one of the first cities to use electricity in Washington. John Shoudy built the plant in the 1887 but sold it to the city in 1890 for $34,000. It was the main source of electricity for Ellensburg until 1951, when the city began buying power from the Bonneville Power Administration.

The Ellensburg Woolen Mill, built in 1912, was an investment venture with hopes of processing the wool from the large numbers of sheep in the valley. The woolen mill failed after a few years, and the building was used for the Kittitas County Fair in the 1920s before the rodeo grounds were built. Later it became the headquarters and sawmill for the Boise Cascade Lumber Company. In the 1970s, the building closed, and today it houses Inland Boat and Motor.

The Cadwell-Olymic Block on the northwest corner of Fourth Avenue and Pearl Street is pictured here around 1900. At the far right, toward the end of the road, is the Horton Hotel. The Horton was the nicest hotel of the time and had a cupola of its own on the corner. The cupola came down, but the building remained a hotel until the 1960s.

Cor. 4th + Pearl
Ellensburg

Fashion Stables, which were located at 207 North Main Street, are shown here in 1913. In 1908, brothers B. T. and W. D. Larsen took charge of the Fashion Stables, operating under the firm name of the Larsen Brothers. B. T. Larsen was the manager in active charge of the business, and his brother lived in North Yakima, where he was a veterinarian. B. T. Larsen was also a veterinarian and did much along those lines in Ellensburg. The Larsen brothers's sister, Margaret, was married to A. J. Splawn.

This photograph shows the Clarence Palmer Livery Stables on the northwest corner of Sixth Avenue and Main Street around 1900. Palmer bought out McGrath early on and moved to this new location, which he operated out of for many years. When the automobile began to replace the horse, Palmer was quick to change with the times. He converted his livery into an automobile storage and taxi, and also sold gasoline to customers. The more recent picture (below), taken in 1925, shows Clarence Palmer on the far right and his fleet of cars and drivers. Palmer sold out in the 1940s, and Jack Spence operated Spence's Service Station, which later became Spence's Texaco Station, on this location for many more years.

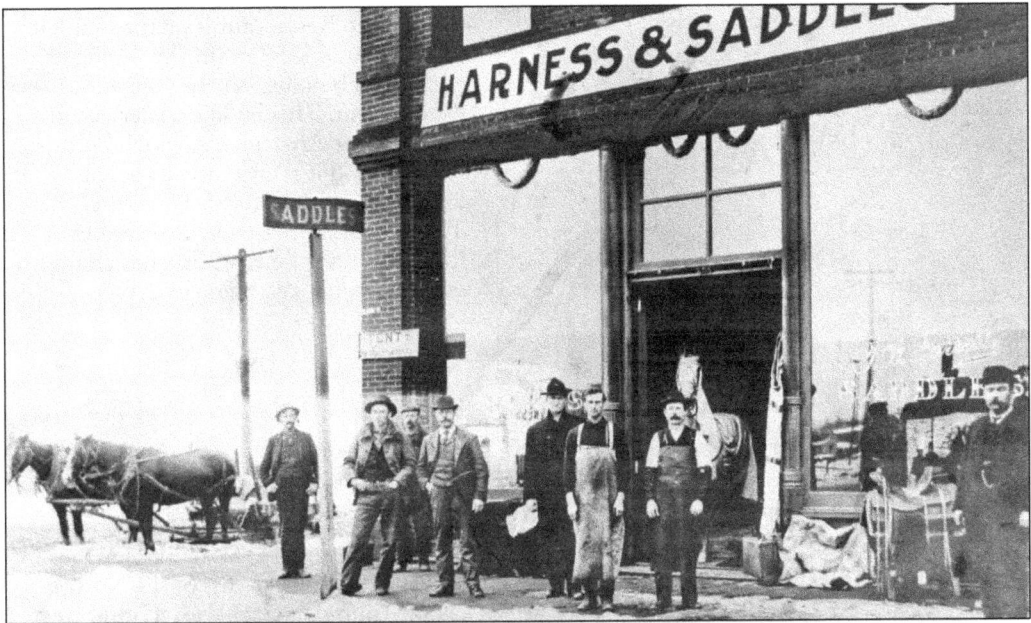

T. W. Farrell's Harness and Saddle store at 301 North Main Street is shown here in a photograph taken before 1900. Billie Farrell, the owner, is standing in front of the horse. Farrell spoke the Chinook Jargon, and many of his patrons were Native Americans that lived in the valley. This location is the original corner of Ellensburg, and the mannequin horse in the doorway can be seen in the Kittitas County Historical Museum today.

The New York Store is pictured here around 1911. H. L. Stowell (standing, second from right) and his son Charles Scudder Stowell (standing, left) are in front of their store, just east of the Davidson Building on the north side of Fourth Avenue between Pearl and Pine Streets. This building is the Elmira Block, which was built just after the fire of 1889. H. L. Stowell owned the building.

The Palace Restaurant is pictured at left in its original location in the Blumauer and Webb building on the east side of Main Street. This building later became the Webster Apartments, which burned in 1986, and it is currently a vacant lot just south of Fitterer's Furniture. The restaurant has moved to various locations over the years and has changed ownership, but the name lives on.

Moore's Lodging House, which was located a few blocks east of the Northern Pacific train depot on West Third Street, is shown below as it appeared around 1895. There were several lodging houses along Third Avenue that hoped to catch the attention of weary train travelers as they walked from the depot toward downtown.

The interior of the Boss Bakery and Gilmour Grocery is pictured here in a photograph taken around 1908. Fred Gilmour is on the left behind the counter, and Layman Bolyard is the man standing on the far right. The man in the middle is unidentified. The store was in the Boss Bakery building, constructed by Frank Bossong, on the west side of Pearl Street between Third and Fourth Avenues.

Kelleher Motors and Garage is shown here in the early 1930s. Jack Kelleher immigrated to the United States with his mother from Dublin, Ireland as a boy and came to Ellensburg in 1905. He opened a bicycle shop in 1907, but in 1911, he decided to get into the automobile business and began the Kelleher Motor Company. Jack died in 1950, but his family still operates Kelleher Ford, which has always been in the same location.

Lou Bender is behind the counter of the Lobby Pool Hall around 1912. Bender came to Ellensburg in 1899 at age 19. He worked for Clarence Palmer's livery stable and then as a freight hauler in the valley. Later Bender opened the Lobby Pool Hall in the Lyons Building on Third Avenue, which he ran for five years before selling it. The pool hall offered beer, cigars, and billiards, and was a popular spot for years.

Above is the Pearson Building, constructed in 1908, on the southwest corner of Fourth and Main Streets. Samuel Pearson, a prominent business owner, constructed this building, which housed the newly formed Elks Lodge on the second floor. This early-20th-century photograph shows the transition from horse transportation to the automobile, with a bicycle visible leaning against the building. The Pearson Building houses the Palace Café today.

In this view of the Davidson Building, taken around 1910, the popular Hotel Savoy occupied the second floor and offered guests transportation in the horse-drawn taxi to the train depot as well as tours around town. The Elmira Building, which housed the New York Store, is on the right, and the G. R. Stewart Building is on the left. On the first floor of the Davidson Building was Lauderdale's clothier, as well as a barbershop.

The Ellensburg City Council passed a resolution in 1908 that secured a $10,000 grant from Andrew Carnegie to build a free public library in the city. The stipulation was that the city had to levy a "free library fund" in the amount of $1,000 per year for upkeep of the new building. The library was completed in 1910, and the first librarian was Jean Davidson. The building was torn down in the summer of 1967, and the new public library was built in its place.

The Webster Hotel on the southwest corner of Third Avenue and Pearl Street was constructed in 1909 by G. A. Knox for the Ellensburg Brewing and Malting Company. The structure, built of brick for hotel purposes, cost an estimated $16,000 to complete. It was to be 60 feet by 85 feet and two stories high with the option of adding a third story if desired. Opening in November 1909, the new building was called the Majestic Hotel. Ownership of the hotel changed twice. Then, in 1913, Frank Groger of Seattle purchased the building. He completely remodeled the structure, interior and exterior, including the addition of a third story. The remodeled building was called the Saint Regis Hotel. In July 1937, William Webster purchased the hotel for $20,000 and renamed it the Webster Hotel. During the early morning hours of February 1, 1980, the old hotel was completely destroyed by fire.

In 1905, the Union Fish Market, operated by Luther "Lute" A. Jungst, was located on the northeast corner of Fourth Avenue and Pine Street. The building survived the fire of 1889 and was one of the oldest standing wooden buildings in town. The building was moved to the corner of South Pine Street and Capitol Avenue, and has been drastically remodeled into a house.

The Ellensburg Steam Laundry is shown here around 1905. In a list of town needs, generated by the *Ellensburg Capital* newspaper in 1900, the need for a steam laundry was at the top. William F. Doughty filled that need when he opened the Ellensburg Steam Laundry not long after the article appeared. Doughty was the owner and operator of the laundry, which was located in the City Hall Building at 304 North Pine Street.

Otto Pautzke poses with his studio car on Pearl Street. Pautzke was born on November 15, 1863, in Pomerania, Prussia, and immigrated to the United States with his parents when he was four years old. He grew up in Wisconsin and Minnesota, where he married Ellen Elizabeth Clayton in 1887. Pautzke lived in Minnesota and the Dakotas before he moved west to Slaughter (present-day Auburn), Washington. In Slaughter, Pautzke opened his first photography studio and took pictures of early south King County. In 1896–1897, the Pautzkes moved to Ellensburg with their four children, where Otto Pautzke set up a photography studio. From 1897 until his death in 1918, Pautzke took hundreds of photographs of Ellensburg and the Kittitas Valley, as well as studio portraits of many people. Pautzke's photographic contribution is an invaluable visual record of the early history of the Kittitas Valley.

From a second-floor window of the Washington National Bank building, formerly the Ben Snipes Bank, this photograph was taken looking west down Fourth Avenue at the intersection of Fourth and Pearl Streets. Many local farmers and ranchers ventured into town to purchase supplies and catch up on area news on a wintery Saturday in 1901. Most of the men and boys rode in wagons with attached runners that made for easy pulling by a team of horses.

Above is the Ellensburg National Bank on the southeast corner of Fifth Avenue and Pearl Street before the fire of 1889. This brick building was constructed in 1888 by Edward P. Cadwell and retained its brick exterior until 1930. In 1930, the National Bank of Ellensburg changed the building from brick to art deco. The City of Ellensburg purchased the building in 1937 and ran it as city hall for many years.

Built shortly after the fire of 1889, this lodging house was purchased by Frederick Borrows before 1913. Called the Borrows House, then the Borrow Hotel, and finally the Miller Hotel, it operated until the 1950s. During Prohibition in the 1920s, the "Old Brick" was a thriving speakeasy. The mayor or sheriff would tip them off before a raid, so they had time to hide the liquor and bring out the coffee.

Oil-well rig operating ¼ mile east of Fairview Hall on Fred Schnebly Ranch. circa 1900 to 1910.

An oil rig was set up on the Schnebly Ranch northeast of Ellensburg during the early part of the 20th century. Oil was found on the property, but it did not amount to much. In the 1950s, the Sunshine Oil Company also attempted to find oil near this area but had little success. Again, in the 1970s and 1980s, various companies returned looking for oil and natural gas but had results similar to their predecessors.

The east side of Pine Street between Fourth and Fifth Avenues is pictured here in 1913. The *Ellensburg Dawn* was a local newspaper begun in 1894 by editor Robert A. Turner that lasted for about 20 years. On the first floor was a shoe repair business operated by John R. Smith. The Empire Furniture Company, past the feed store, was operated by J. C. Bench and Son.

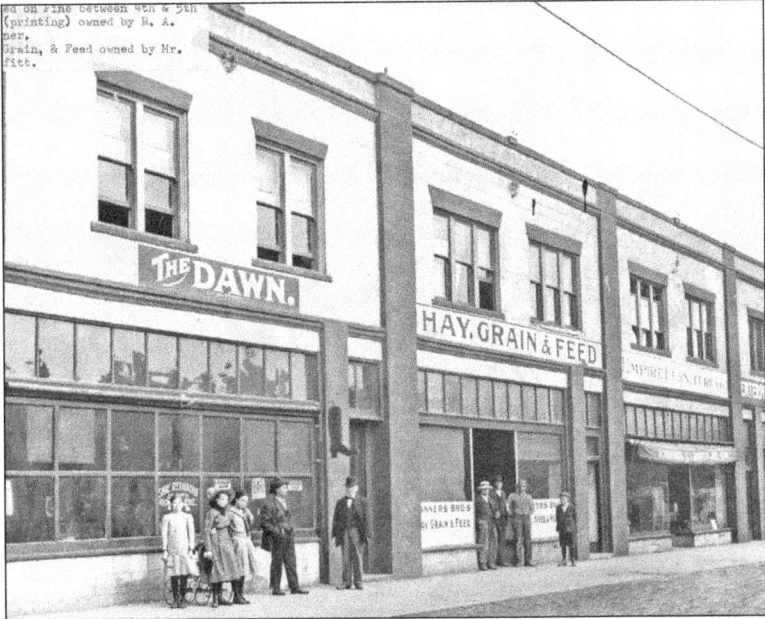

The Ellensburg Telephone Company operators are shown working the switchboard on the first floor of the Masonic Temple on Sixth Avenue in 1928. John Faust bought the Sunset Telephone and Telegraph Company around 1908 and operated it out of the Masonic Temple until 1946, when it was moved into an old building on the corner of Third Avenue and Ruby Street. The Masons currently lease this space to a health food store.

Gerrit d'Ablaing is shown here (left) in front of his real estate office in the Ben Snipes Bank building around 1894. By the door is Judge James G. Boyle, who was a good friend of d'Ablaing and who wrote real estate abstracts for him. Gerrit d'Ablaing was born into Dutch nobility, and came to Ellensburg in 1880 to check on his brother-in-law's financial dealings. d'Ablaing purchased land on the southeast corner of Maple and Manitoba Streets, and built this beautiful home (shown below) in 1881. He married Maude Painter and raised his family in this home. A prominent citizen and an avid local historian, he spent much time recording Ellensburg's events during this early period. d'Ablaing died in 1950, and this house sat abandoned for several years until the Ellensburg Fire Department burned it for practice. The site of this home and its surrounding land was donated to the city to construct Mountain View Park on South Maple Street. A large swing set now sits about where this glorious house once stood.

Four

SCHOOL, CHURCH, AND
COMMUNITY

Denmark School No. 12 was located southeast of Ellensburg in a field owned by the Clerf family. In 1891, William Crowley was the first teacher with 42 students. In the fall of each year, a community fair was held in the school building. This 1898 photograph shows the outhouse, the storage shed, and open barns for horses and buggies to the right of the schoolhouse.

Colockum School District No. 19 gathers here in a photograph taken around 1890. From left to right are Dick Courtway, Gene Courtway, George Cooke, Carrie King (Fulwiler), Nellie King, a Mrs. Whitelsie (teacher), Edna Haley, Mamie Ingersoll, Lila Ingersoll, Fred Ingersoll, Ida Cooke, Bob Ingersoll, Rex Shamley, Harr Ingersoll, Fred Courtway, and Edward Cooke. The Colockum School District was absorbed by Kittitas School District No. 403 in the late 1940s.

The 19 pupils and their teacher pose for this picture on the porch of the Broadview School in 1919. Most of these one-room schoolhouses did not have electricity, which is why they had tall windows. Class was scheduled so the students had time to travel in daylight hours. This school was located south of Ellensburg and was consolidated into the Ellensburg School District in 1942.

The Ellensburg Public School, known both as the Washington and the Central Public School, was built on East Fifth Avenue between Sprague and Anderson Streets. The building was begun in July 1890. The architect was Willis A. Ritchie of Seattle, and the contract was awarded to John Scott of Ellensburg for $38,650. The city traded what was the City Park Block to the school district, and the Ellensburg City Council appropriated $1,000 for the clock in the tower. The new school was open for use in September 1891 and taught all grades. Additionally, when the Washington State Normal School (today's Central Washington University) began in 1891, it had no building of its own, so it used four classrooms in the public school. The state did not pay rent, but it did share the cost of fuel and electricity with the public school. The public school shared space with the normal school until 1894, when the normal school received a building of its own.

The inside of a classroom in the public school is shown here in this photograph from February 1896. Compared to rural one-room schoolhouses, the Ellensburg Public School was luxurious. It had electric lights in the classrooms, and it offered steam-heated rooms, a far cry from the warmth of a woodstove in the rural schoolhouses. The teacher stands at the back of the room, which contains more than 60 pupils at their desks.

The Ellensburg Public School, with the entire student and teacher population, posed for this photograph likely at the end of the school year, around 1895. This school taught students from first grade through high school and was the only school in town until 1908, when the Lourdes Catholic School was built. The impressive building sat three blocks southwest of the normal school's Barge Hall building.

This unique view shows the north side of the public school building, taken from the normal school's Barge Hall, before 1900. North Sprague Street is on the right while the future North Anderson Street, on the left, was still a trail that ended at the Ellensburg Public School. The clock tower had a large bell that sounded on the hour, which many people in town used to set their clocks and watches.

The Washington State Normal School faculty is shown here in 1900. From left to right are (first row) Laura Riddell, Ida Remele, Pres. William E. Wilson, Colena Dickey, and Jessie Wilcox; (second row) Mary Grupe, Prof. John Henry Morgan, ? Miller, Dr. John Munson, unidentified, and Prof. Edwin J. Saunders. Shortly after this picture was taken, Professor Saunders left the normal school to teach chemistry at Harvard.

The large four-story, brick Barge Hall, built in 1893–1894, was the first and only building on the Washington State Normal School campus for the first 18 years of its existence. Classrooms and offices for the entire student and faculty population, plus all the administrative operations, were in this one building. The building was never used for living quarters, so students either had to live close by or room with a family and do work in exchange for a place to sleep. The grand 152-by-120-foot building, constructed by the H. A. Van Fossen Company for $60,000, was designed by Eugene C. Prince. The building superintendent was John Nash, who oversaw the construction of the four-story, stone and wood building, which has an impressive 120-foot-tall bell tower. The bricks used in the construction were made by the A. O. Fowler Brickyard in Ellensburg, which averaged 20,000 bricks per day. The massive sandstone blocks were from the Tenino Sandstone Quarry in Tenino, Washington.

The faculty of the normal school was photographed on the stage in the assembly room in Barge Hall around 1900. Pres. William Wilson is sitting in the middle by the desk onstage. The only faculty member not on stage is Dr. John P. Munson. The assembly room was on the second floor directly above the gymnasium toward the back of the building.

This photograph, taken before 1900, faces south at the Washington State Normal School's Barge Hall (left) and the Ellensburg Public School building (right) on Fifth Avenue. The two buildings stood ominously in the small town, by far the two biggest structures in the whole valley. The picture was taken from a private residence that is now university property near Hebeler Hall's present-day location.

67

Prominent Ellensburg photographer Otto Pautzke took this beautiful panoramic picture of the north half of Ellensburg from the west side of Craig's Hill in 1898. The Washington Public School (left) was built in 1890 and taught all the primary and secondary grades. Three years later, Barge Hall (right) was built on Eighth Avenue and opened as the Washington State Normal School.

These two giants were the educational centers of the community and stood like silent giants over the small town. This picture also shows what the residential part of early Ellensburg looked like, including outhouses, barns, and horses where neighborhoods now stand. To the right of Barge Hall is Mount Stewart.

Pictured here is Barge Hall as seen from Anderson Street around 1902. Black smoke is visible coming out of the chimney, and ivy covers the walls around the main entrance. Barge Hall sat alone on campus for many years until the student population began to outgrow the single building. Also with the rising student population came the need for some sort of student housing.

Shown here are Barge Hall and the new Education Training School on D Street, which was built in 1908. The named was changed to Edison Hall in 1917, but it continued as an elementary school for selected area children and for preparing the normal school students to become teachers. In 1939, a new and improved college elementary school was built, and Edison Hall became the school's music building. Edison Hall was demolished in 1987.

Young students of the normal school's Edison Elementary are shown here on campus in the early part of the 20th century. The teacher was Clara Meisner, who was the kindergarten-primary supervisor from 1906–1938. Meisner taught German at the normal school and kindergarten classes, and coordinated much of the training program on campus. It was through Meisner's efforts that public funds were designated to establish kindergarten programs in the state of Washington. Meisner died in 1938, but in 1966, the college named a new 125-bed dormitory after her in a dedication ceremony. Meisner Hall is still part of the Bassetties Complex of dorms on campus.

This picture, taken before 1900, shows an art classroom in Barge Hall on the Washington State Normal School Campus. The normal school taught a wide variety of topics since it trained teachers in most every discipline. Two students work on different projects as the instructor looks on from her desk.

Built in 1911 as the first girl's dormitory on the campus of the Washington State Normal School, Kamola Hall was constructed with locally made bricks. The building's namesake was the daughter of the famous Kittitas Indian chief Owhi. An addition was built in 1915 that increased accommodations to satisfy 112 students. Since 1974, the hall has been coed.

This Otto Pautzke photograph of the students and faculty of the Washington State Normal School was taken on June 28, 1915. The building on the right is Barge Hall, the main building on campus. The three-story building was the science and education building, which has since been removed. Between the two buildings is Kamola Hall, the first and only dormitory on campus at the time. (Courtesy of Patrick Stanton.)

Barge Hall, Edison Hall, and the old science and education building, located on the normal school campus, are shown here in 1916. Just out of view to the right was Kamola Hall, the girls' dorm. Tuition was free at the school, and the only fee was a $10 library fee, half of which would be refunded if it was not used. Room and board at Kamola Hall was $4 per week.

A horse-powered road crew grades Eighth Avenue (University Way) near the intersection of Eighth and D Street around 1910. Barge Hall and Edison Hall can be seen in the background. The wooden crosswalk was located where the current crosswalk is at this intersection. The Ellensburg City Council voted to grade the streets in the northwest part of the city in August 1910, appropriating $6,750 for the work.

Leafless trees surround Barge Hall, and dark smoke rises from the main chimney on a cold winter day in 1902. A large residential house located in the open fields behind Barge Hall can be seen in the background. The smoke is from the large coal furnace that heated the building's many rooms.

Located on North Pine Street between Seventh and Eighth Avenues was the Lourdes Academy and the Saint Andrews Catholic Church. The church was built in 1884 and was moved to this location in 1904. The academy was completed in the fall of 1908. It was used as a school for Catholic children but also housed a convent and provided living quarters for students. The building was discontinued as a school in 1966 when the property was sold. Lourdes Academy is on the right and Saint Andrews Catholic Church is on the left facing North Pine Street. In 1966, Albertson's Grocery bought the land and demolished the buildings to construct their new store.

D 3897   Lourdes Academy, Ellensburg, Wash.

Morgan Middle School was built in 1929 to house the junior high students that had been displaced by the public school building fire. Morgan was built facing the Ellensburg High School, and the two schools shared facilities. The high school used the Morgan Auditorium, and the junior high used the cafeteria in the high school. Morgan expanded its building, and the high school moved to its present location.

This picture was taken of the east side and main entrance of the Ellensburg High School, which was built in 1912 on South Sprague Street. The building was last used as a high school during the 1955–1956 school year. For a few years, the building remained empty except for use by the staff and students of Morgan junior high. The old school was eventually used as a school storage facility until it was demolished in 1991.

The public school building was destroyed by fire in 1924, displacing many students who attended junior high and elementary school there. This picture was taken shortly after the fire, which gutted the old building and burned the clock tower. The displaced students had to be farmed out to churches, rural schoolhouses, and meeting halls until a new elementary school building was built.

Although the city had three elementary schools by the 1950s, there were still several rural schoolhouses that taught elementary students. Here the students of the Reecer Creek Grade School pose with their teacher, Florence Dearing, at the end of the 1949–1950 school year. These rural schools only taught elementary, so the children had to come to town for secondary education.

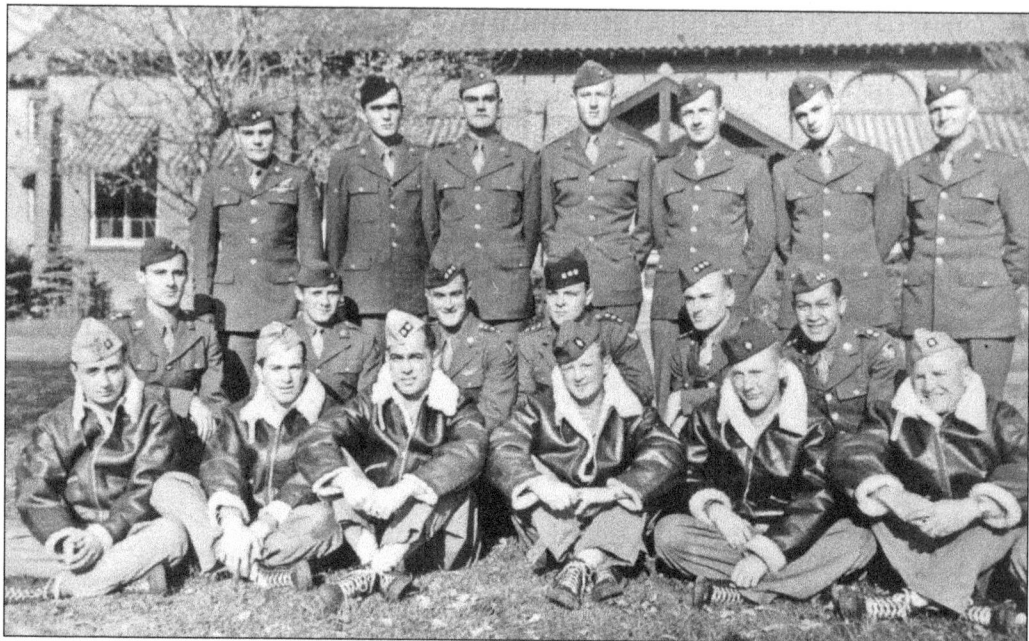

During World War II, the Central Washington College of Education (CWCE)—formerly the Washington State Normal School—became the location of a training school for the U.S. Army Air Force Corps. The school and airport were used to instruct the 314th Cadet training detachment. This group picture was taken in 1943 in front of Sue Lombard Hall, which housed the men while on campus.

This picture was taken in September 1942 and shows the airmen attending the CWCE for pilot training. In the second row are the various student pilots. On the left in the first row are pilot instructors, and on the far right were the CWCE ground instructors.

The pilot trainees are shown here in a classroom in 1942 as part of the cadet flying program with CWCE. Mac Anderson, sitting in front of the window, was the manager of the program. The future pilots took classes by Bower's Field north of Ellensburg; they also did their flight training there.

Above is an aerial view of Bower's Field Airport, located north of Ellensburg, during the World War II cadet training program. The airport was much smaller than this in the 1930s, but leading into and during World War II, Ellensburg was picked as one of a few inland locations for an air base. Work began, and soon the small airstrip was converted into this large airport.

The cornerstone of the First Methodist Episcopal Church was laid in 1891, and the church building and parsonage was completed in 1893. This large and inspiring building replaced a small one-room church that was destroyed by the 1889 fire. A grant of $1,500 was secured from the Methodist Extension for building the new church on the northeast corner of North Ruby Street and Third Avenue. A beautifully toned bell, costing $1,200, was brought by horse and wagon from The Dalles, Oregon, and was placed in the tall steeple. The parsonage on the right was built during the ministry of Pastor Nathan Evans. This building lasted until the 1920s, when a new two-story brick Methodist church was built across the street. The Methodists moved into their new location on July 31, 1921, and still meet there today.

The First Christian Church of Ellensburg was established in 1882 by Keithly Bailes, a pioneer circuit-rider preacher. The present two-story, brick structure, located on the northeast corner of Ruby Street and Sixth Avenue, was erected in 1919 during the ministry of F. E. Billington. This building replaced the original wooden church.

The First Presbyterian Church, located at 406 North Sprague Street is shown here. Originally the Ellensburg Academy building, it was moved to this location in 1899, and a large sanctuary was added. The new church was dedicated on September 24, 1899, and Rev. James A. Laurie was given the bell by his classmates from Williams College. This building was used until 1958, when it was torn down and the church moved to a new location.

Looking south down Sprague Street at the intersection of Fourth Avenue, the original First Baptist Church can be seen. After the establishment of a Baptist church in Ellensburg in 1887, the First Baptist Church building was erected in 1888–1889. The cost of the construction was $3,000. In 1944, a disastrous fire destroyed the old church, which was soon replaced by a large stone and brick structure.

The small wooden Grace Episcopal Church, located on the northwest corner of North Sprague Street and Fourth Avenue, served church members from 1897 to 1964. Rev. Charles L. W. Reese stands on the entry steps of the church with two young boys, and a woman with a baby carriage is on the sidewalk. The rectory and parish house sat to the left of the church. The church was torn down to make room for a Safeway grocery.

The 1912–1913 Ellensburg YMCA basketball team poses for the camera. The Ellensburg chapter of the Young Men's Christian Association (YMCA) began in 1911 on the northwest corner of Fourth Avenue and Pearl Street. The YMCA was deeply involved in the community and offered many activities for young men in town. The Ellensburg YMCA closed in 1965 due to financial problems.

Ellensburg baseball player Jim Pautzke poses for his father, Otto Pautzke, in the family studio on Pearl Street. During this time, there were several baseball teams in town. The high school and Catholic school had teams. In addition, an Ellensburg Baseball Association was formed, and the team played on a field west of the Northern Pacific train depot. They played teams from Seattle, North Yakima, and Roslyn for a few years.

Four women enjoy a typical winter day in Ellensburg ice-skating on Sander's Pond in 1905. The pond was on Carl A. Sander's property, two miles northeast of town. Sander built the pond on Wilson Creek and opened a gristmill in 1886. Pioneer Frederick Ludi lived with the Sander family when he retired. Pictured from left to right are Mrs. Louis "Frances" Sharp, Anna Sander, Bertha Stauffer, and Mabel Sander.

A group of nicely dressed people is out for a Sunday drive to the city well, west of downtown Ellensburg near the Yakima River. The city well was built in 1912 and provided water for businesses and citizens in the city that did not have their own wells. This system still works; today the City of Ellensburg's water supply comes from seven wells.

Pres. William Howard Taft's tour of the West stopped in Ellensburg on September 15, 1909. Taft was riding the Northern Pacific Railway line, stopping in various towns and giving speeches. When the residents of Ellensburg heard he would be passing through, they set to work building a large stage made out of straw bales for the president to speak from. They put the stage just east of the Northern Pacific depot on Third Avenue. When Taft arrived, he was surprised to see the stage and commented that he was not expecting to make a speech in Ellensburg. Taft made an impromptu speech that was punctuated with comments on the region and agriculture. Many people missed the speech; however, because the town was told Taft would arrive at 3:20 p.m., but he arrived at 2:30 p.m. After the speech, Taft commented on the uniqueness of the stage and left for Seattle.

Ellensburg pioneers participate in a Fourth of July parade in 1911 in this photograph, taken near the corner of Fifth Avenue and Main Street. They were guests of Clarence Palmer Livery and Stables, which placed its best hackney carriage and its $700 black coach team—said to be one of the finest in the state—at their disposal. Among those pictured are Sylvanius Ray Geddis (1838–1912), seated beside the driver; Peter McClary (1821–1917), standing on the left; James Ferguson (1839–1917), standing at right; Frederick Ludi (1831–1916), seated on the left; Tilman Houser (1840–1918), seated center; and Jesse McDonald (1831–1917), seated on the right. Frederick Ludi arrived in the valley in 1868 and Tilman Houser in 1869. The other four men followed within the next few years. Less than seven years after this picture was taken, all the men had passed away.

Pres. Theodore Roosevelt stopped in Ellensburg to give a speech on May 25, 1903. Roosevelt was on a train tour in the West and made a scheduled stop in Ellensburg while traveling to Seattle. His train arrived at 9:00 a.m. to a welcome of deafening cheers from the thousands who gathered at the chance to see the president. Newspaper reports claim that nearly 6,000 people turned out to see Roosevelt, many packing themselves together by the Northern Pacific depot and others clamoring onto buildings to get a better view. A procession of schoolchildren—led by Civil War and Spanish-American War veterans—and a band marched to the depot to welcome the president. Roosevelt stepped onto a decorated platform just outside the depot and delivered a speech about how to be better Americans by being more morally, socially, financially, and intellectually aware. After thanking the crowd, Roosevelt reboarded his train car and left the depot for Seattle.

The local Elks lodge met in the Samuel Pearson building on Main Street from their inception in 1908 until the construction of their own building. The Benevolent and Protective Order of Elks (BPOE) building, known as the Elks's Temple, on the northeast corner of Fifth and Main Streets, was built in 1923 by the local Elks chapter for $56,000. The Ellensburg Elks Lodge committee consisted of Julius Caesar Hubbell, Rodney Palmer, Robert Turner, and other well-respected men in the city. McWilliams and Ross of Yakima, Washington, were the general contractors. The marble cornerstone was donated by the Puget Sound Marble Company. When the building was dedicated in March 1923, there was a big celebration by the Elks members. This car was part of the dedication ceremony, adorned with an Elk's head on the front and decorations along the sides.

Looking north on Pearl Street under the large evergreen arch located in the center of the intersection of Pearl Street and Fourth Avenue, the Davidson Building can be seen on the right. The large evergreen arch was built by community and fraternal organizations to celebrate the return of Company H (mostly Kittitas County men) from the Philippines at the end of the Spanish-American War on November 11, 1899.

On January 15, 1920, at the Elks lodge meeting room in the Pearson Building, the patrons met for one last drink. The next day, Prohibition became law, which made the manufacture, sale, transport, and consumption of alcohol illegal. These partygoers celebrated their last night of legal debauchery and, from the wording of the signs on the walls, took it all in stride.

The Knights Templar stood in full regalia in front of the Ellensburg Masonic Temple on Sixth Avenue around 1909. The Ellensburg Masons were established in February 1882, and many of the early prominent settlers and businessmen were Masons. They met first in the Odd Fellows Hall and then in the Johnson House Hotel on Pearl Street. The Ellensburg Elks Lodge had their own building constructed on the northwest corner of Fourth Avenue and Pine Street, but it burned in the fire of 1889. Immediately following the fire, the lodge moved to build a new temple while temporarily meeting in the Nash Building. The Masons constructed their new temple on Sixth Avenue and moved in at the end of 1890. After some economic hardship, undoubtedly spurred on by the Panic of 1893, the Masons lost the deed to their temple in 1897. They continued to meet but at a separate location until 1908, when they finally repurchased the deed and moved back into their building permanently. The Ellensburg Masons still meet in this historic building. (Courtesy of the Ellensburg Masons.)

Five

FAIR AND RODEO

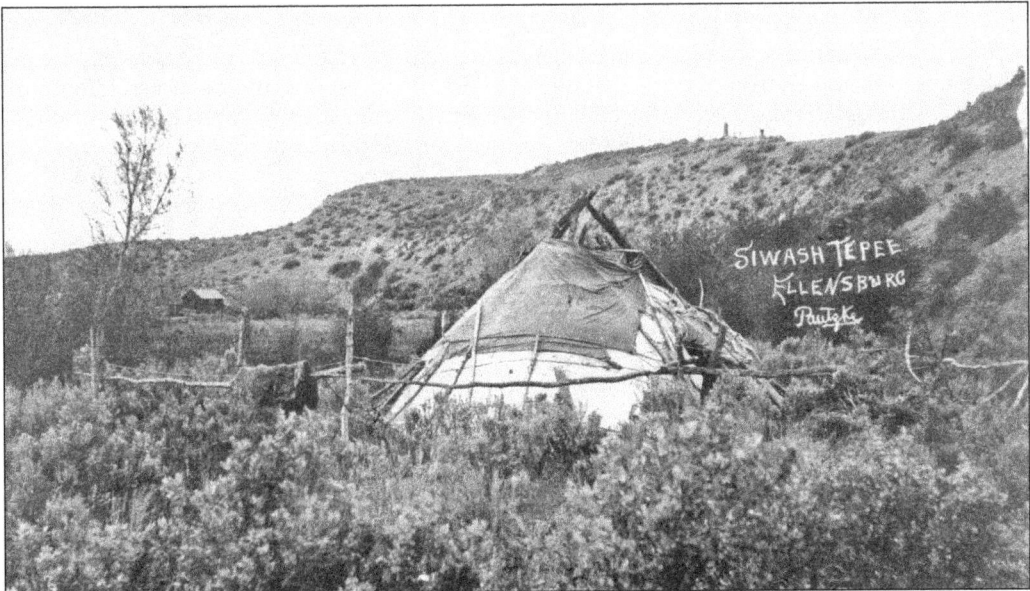

Owhi's daughter Old Julie's tepee was located on the future site of the fair and rodeo grounds, shown here in this c. 1910 Otto Pautzke photograph. Before settlers came to the valley, the Kittitas band of the Yakama Indians had a large camp at this location. The Yakama Indians still set up their tepees during the rodeo each year, a symbolic reminder of their history in the valley.

This picture was taken from the top of Craig's Hill looking west toward downtown Ellensburg in 1900. Although hard to see, Barge Hall on the normal school campus and the public school building on Fifth Avenue can both be seen, on the right and left, respectively. The fence-lined open area in the foreground is the current site of the Ellensburg Rodeo arena and the Kittitas

County Fair. The long fence, extending toward the photographer on the left, would run directly though the rodeo arena if it were still standing. Pioneer dairyman B. F. Reed donated the sagebrush-covered hillside and a couple of lots to the county. The rest of the land was purchased for $6,450 from private owners.

In 1922, Kittitas County official Leonard Davis suggested that Ellensburg should build a fairground to show off local agriculture. Davis had University of Washington landscape artist Dean James Gould draw up a plan for a fair and rodeo ground, and took it to the Ellensburg Chamber of Commerce. J. C. "Cliff" Kaynor presided over the chamber, and the plan was approved. They began acquiring the land for the new location and decided that the bulk of the work, which was land clearing and grading, would be done by volunteers from the community. On June 14, 1923, more than 500 men arrived to work, and over 100 women volunteered food and services. This view shows the massive volunteer effort by the community that day that converted the sage land to a fair and rodeo ground in a matter of days.

Land for a new rodeo ground at the base of Craig's Hill is graded in this picture, taken on June 14, 1923. Of the 500 volunteers that showed up, 300 were farmers who brought their own equipment and horses. Over half the volunteers camped overnight and continued working the next day. The other 200 were local businessmen.

Horses, gas-powered machines, and brute strength were all used in the massive effort to clear the grounds to get the location ready for the construction of a grandstand, fences, and corrals. Local cattleman Lou Richards, who later became the arena director, was put in charge of organizing the workers. Richards was an integral part of the rodeo from the beginning, and he later served as the Kittitas County commissioner. County engineer Warren Bowman was put in charge of task planning, which included the daunting tasks of moving Wilson Creek and also ensuring that the surveying of the grounds matched the layout plans. This view looks north at the progress of the volunteer work during what was dubbed "field day." Local businesses closed during the field day to encourage everyone to support the effort. The 18-acre site was to include a one third–mile circumference racetrack with an athletic field in the middle that could be used for the rodeo as well as other sporting events.

Pautzke Photo

The completed work was ready for its first fair and rodeo by September 1923, less than 90 days from the beginning of ground clearing. Dr. Hubert E. Pfenning, a local veterinarian and community leader, was the first to suggest having some sort of Wild West show or rodeo-type attraction at the fair. After the work was underway, Pfenning was put in charge of securing stock and cowboys for the first rodeo in 1923. Pfenning traveled to a rodeo in Ephrata, Washington, in the summer of 1923 and had cowboys sign contracts that would guarantee their participation. Pfenning also used his ties as a veterinarian to contact horse owners in the area, who provided the horses for the rodeo. As a side note, across the arena in the distance is the public school, which would be destroyed by fire less than a year after this picture was taken.

This view shows the Kittitas County Fair's new home next to the rodeo arena. In the lower right corner is a makeshift carousel for children. The large building in the middle was where the agricultural and craft exhibits were located. For the first few years of the fair, there were not many buildings because the organizers were not sure how successful it would be.

Fifteen years after inception, the Kittitas County Fair and Ellensburg Rodeo still looked much the same but had grown considerably. The rodeo added more seating by extending the covered grandstand and adding a small grandstand on the hillside made from the flat timber bottoms of old train cars. The fair changed more as many new buildings were added, and the Native American tepee village encompassed half a city block.

An important staple of the fair and rodeo is the Rodeo Parade, which winds its way through downtown Ellensburg. Here the Ellensburg Fire Department leads the parade south on Pearl Street between Fourth and Fifth Avenues in the 1940s. The Cadwell-Olympic Block building is on the left, which was built after the 1889 fire but was demolished in 1979 after suffering its own fire.

This aerial view looks north toward the fair and rodeo in 1932. The Vista House, which sits on the edge of Craig's Hill, serves as the American Legion Hall. In the rodeo arena, the hash mark lines of a football field can be seen. As soon as the arena was built, the normal and high school began using it for their athletic events, as did a local polo association.

A picture captures the inside of the rodeo arena during the grand entry where various riders carry flags that represent their organization or that specify a sponsor's name. Looking northeast, the original bucking chutes can be seen on the left. Also note the grass infield of the arena, which was used by the college and high school football teams until 1957.

An unidentified saddle bronc rider holds on at an early Ellensburg rodeo above. Cars line the edge of Craig's Hill, dubbed "free-loader" hill because of the free view it has of the events. The crowd of people on the hillside sat on the additional grandstands added after the first rodeo in 1923. The other men on horses are there to provide help if the cowboy should need it.

Mabel Strickland is shown here calf roping at an early Ellensburg rodeo. Strickland was petite, pretty, and appeared very dainty, yet she was an expert horse rider and a great calf roper who could hold her own against the top cowboys of the day. Mabel married bronc rider and calf roper Hugh Strickland in 1918 when she was 21. During the 1920s, she excelled in trick riding, calf roping, steer riding, and horse racing. Mabel garnered national press, and her appearance at various rodeos received more attention than most of the cowboys. She is the only woman to ever appear on the cover of the Cheyenne Frontier Days program. In the 1930s, Mabel was recognized by Hollywood, where she performed in movies and did stunt work. Mabel retired from movies and rodeos in 1941, settling on her Arizona farm and raising appaloosa horses. She passed away in 1976 and has been posthumously inducted into nearly every cowboy and cowgirl hall of fame.

People dance at the rodeo kickoff breakfast, then called the Booster Breakfast, which was held on Pearl Street between Fourth and Fifth Avenues. Behind the dancers, a breakfast of sausage, eggs, and buttermilk pancakes was served. The Ellensburg Chamber of Commerce served a free Western breakfast and provided entertainment two weeks before the rodeo began as a way to get locals excited about the coming rodeo and fair.

The Yakama Indians ride horses on the track while a band plays in the rodeo arena during an early rodeo. The Yakamas have always been an important part of the fair and rodeo, and serve as a reminder of Ellensburg's early history. In the distance to the right of the tree is Barge Hall on the normal school campus.

The 1929 Ellensburg Rodeo Queen, Helen Nason (center), her younger sister, Princess Minnie Nason (left), and an unidentified girl pose in the rodeo arena. Both local girls were members of the Yakama Nation, which marks the first time a Native American was crowned Rodeo Queen or Princess in Ellensburg. Helen was a sophomore honor student in Ellensburg High School, and they were the daughters of Ida Joseph Nason.

A stagecoach race makes its way around the track at the 1940 Ellensburg Rodeo. Les and Cecil Taylor are at the helm of the coach on the left, and Bill Heaverlo is cracking the whip on the other coach. The fast paced and dangerous stagecoach races were a popular event at the rodeo each year.

Yakama Indians march in the annual rodeo parade down Pearl Street. This picture was taken from a temporary platform built out of a second-story window in the Davidson Building. The clock on the sidewalk has been a longtime staple downtown. Jeweler Jay N. O. Thomson put the ornate clock in front of his jewelry store, and many people set their watches to it for years.

Fred "Toby" Lugviel holds on tight as the Brahma he is riding leaps completely off the ground at the 1947 rodeo. Interested, fellow cowboys and rodeo fans watch to see if Toby can complete the ride. Lugviel spent much time in Washington, Wyoming, and Oregon riding the rodeo circuit.

Six

AGRICULTURE AND FARMING

From left to right, George, Ben, and Jim Ferguson are pictured here working on Abel Dunning's Ranch in 1910, which was located on Wilson Creek northeast of town. As soon as irrigation water arrived in the valley, farmers began growing hay. The ample sunshine and low humidity made the Kittitas Valley an ideal location to grow hay. These men are cutting the hay, which was baled after given time to dry out.

This c. 1909 photograph is of the Minielly family and the crew they hired to work their farm near Ellensburg. George Minielly emigrated from Canada when he was 19 and worked in different logging camps in Washington. After moving around and working different jobs, he came to Ellensburg in 1896 and purchased a hay press, which he used on the 40 acres of land he purchased in 1899. George married Ellensburg-native Addie Ferguson in 1898, and they had two children, Myrtle, born in 1899, and Stanley, born in 1900. Both children were born on the farm. George is on the left, standing next to Addie, who is sitting on some farm machinery. Myrtle is wearing her white dress, and her brother, Stanley, is sitting behind her. The rest of the men were workers hired by the Minielly family as farm hands and laborers.

Wealthy farmer William T. Sheldon began a 20-acre apple orchard, a small part of his 1,300 acres, in the early part of the 19th century. In 1907, he sold his orchard to Elizabeth B. Loomis, who moved from Tacoma with her two daughters to the valley and began work on the orchard. Elizabeth named the orchard "Shelterneuk," which became a model orchard and was well known for its produce.

A two-row planter is pulled by a tractor on a farm in Badger Pocket in 1932. Before rubber tires, metal tractor wheels had lugs on them that helped with traction. The lead tractor here pulls the machine that planted two rows of seeds at the same time. Before the advent of the tractor, horses were used to pull the planters through the fields.

This picture shows what much of the Kittitas Valley looked like before settlement. In areas where there was no natural water, the ground was covered with the sagebrush seen here. To break the ground took a lot of work since the plants had firm roots in the hard soil. This seven-horse team pulls the plow across the ground in Badger Pocket in 1932.

The Scammon family is shown here on their farm, which was east of Ellensburg, near Kittitas, Washington, around 1908. Robert I. Scammon is on the left, and his wife, Sarah, is on the far right. Between them is their son, Carl, and daughter, Cora Floyd. The Scammon farm raised crops, such as these potatoes, had more than 2,500 head of sheep, and raised horses, some of which were used as bucking horses in the rodeo.

This early picture of a Kittitas Valley threshing crew was taken in 1898. The steam-powered tractor pulled the massive threshing machine and was also used as the power source to run the thresher. The workers fed the grain stalks into the thresher, which separated the grain from the husks and spit the straw aside.

This is a 1912 picture of the Jens Sorenson farm in the Denmark district of the valley. Sorenson emigrated from Denmark in 1881 and came to Ellensburg in 1888, working for the Northern Pacific Railway. In 1892, he purchased this piece of land southeast of town and began building his farm, which included a seven-room house for his family of six children.

A typical hay-baling crew in the Kittitas Valley takes a break for a photograph opportunity. The men in the middle are standing on and around the baler. The haystack is manually fed into the baler, which is powered by the large belt from the tractor behind the car. None of the people are identified, but it appears that the farm owners are in the car, wearing the clean clothes.

The Saint Louis Brewery was established in the 1890s and sat in west Ellensburg just over a mile from town. The brewery used water from a spring-fed well and produced 28 barrels of beer a week to supply the local saloons. In the 1920s, during Prohibition, the brewery ceased making its product. This picture was taken in 1941 long after the brewery closed its doors.

Above is the Damman Flour Mill, which was built west of town in 1879. This mill was the second flour mill in the valley and was first a burr mill. The lumber to build the mill was hauled over the Manastash Ridge from the Wenas Valley. Ellensburg amateur historian photographer Fred Breckon took this picture in 1942 while the mill was still standing.

The men here were haying on the Robbins farm, which was north of Ellensburg in the Reecer Creek district. Charles Robbins is standing atop the huge hay pile, and Lloyd Robbins is standing by the horse. These brothers were two of 14 children born to Dr. John Robbins and his wife, Elizabeth. The large rake was used to lift the cut hay to the top of the pile with the help of some horses.

Dr. John Robbins immigrated to America from England in 1872 with his wife and 12 children in tow. After moving around the country, they decided to settle in Portland. Not content, Robbins and his eldest son came to the Kittitas Valley via horseback from The Dalles, Oregon, in search of better land. When Robbins saw the lush green Kittitas Valley, he decided he wanted to finally settle down and begin a farm. Robbins, his wife, and their children—by then, 14 total—moved to the valley in 1878. Robbins built this home on his land in the Reecer Creek area, about 12 miles north of Ellensburg. Pictured here in 1901, from left to right, are Dr. John Robbins, Old Dick (horse), Clara, Laura, Mary, William (seated), Blanche, and mother Elizabeth. The family farm was run by his sons until 1912, when they sold it and went into the hardware business in Yakima.

The process of threshing grain in the Kittitas Valley is shown here. The large pile on the left was the cut wheat ready to be threshed. The plant was fed into the thresher, which separated the grain (kernels) from the hull. The grain went through the chute and into the bags—the man here is filling the bags. The stem part of the plant was separated to be used as animal feed or straw bedding.

Large-scale hay operations had to protect their product, for it was their livelihood at stake. As daunting as it seems, many farmers would pile their hay bales into massive stacks and then build sheds around them. These buildings, while well-constructed and laboriously built, were often temporary, and many times they were taken down and moved the following year. The advent of tarps removed the need for the temporary buildings, but permanent hay sheds are still a feature in the Kittitas Valley.

Farming in the Kittitas Valley would not have been possible without irrigation water, a problem farmers began solving early on. Some of the first settlers diverted creeks into hand-dug ditches to bring water to their farms. Not long after, irrigation flumes were built to bring a larger supply of water to farmers around Ellensburg. This group poses on a recently constructed irrigation flume outside Ellensburg.

This Pautzke photograph of an irrigation flume was part of the Cascade Canal, which ran parallel to the highway from Cle Elum to Ellensburg. Begun in 1903, the canal was 42 miles long and supplied enough water to irrigate 15,000 acres of farmland. The Cascade Canal took its water from the Yakima River where it enters the Kittitas Valley.

Seven

TRANSPORTATION

Bertha Rehmke (left) and Ellen Pautzke rest with their bicycles on the northeast corner of North Main Street and Sixth Avenue in this c. 1908 Pautzke photograph. Bertha was the wife of well-known Ellensburg businessman William Rehmke, and Ellen was the wife and partner of Otto Pautzke, longtime local photographer. The Pautzkes lived at 608 North Main Street behind the large house on the right.

Crowds of people walk east along Third Avenue from the Northern Pacific Railway depot toward downtown Ellensburg. It was six blocks from the train depot to the major business district of Ellensburg. When the train arrived, hotel carriages provided transportation for visitors and travelers. Small cafes and lodging houses lined Third Street. The R. P. Tjossem and Son warehouse can be seen in center of photograph.

Sven "Sam" Pearson, his wife, Clementine Zilpha, and his stepdaughter, Pearl, were photographed in their new buggy, which was the first with rubber tires in Ellensburg. Pearson immigrated from Sweden and arrived in the Kittitas Valley in 1884. He was a successful businessman, having built the Pearson Building on the southwest corner of Fifth Avenue and Main Street, and had been involved in businesses on several important corners in town.

Saddle maker T. W. "Billy" Farrell and his daughter, Gertrude, ride in a one-horse open sleigh around Christmas time on Pearl Street. The Hotel Washington, located at 317 ½ North Pearl Street, was upstairs, and below it was Schultz's Candy Store. Schultz's store is festively adorned with swags and trees, hoping to lure in Christmas shoppers.

The old Ellensburg Bicycle Company garage, owned by R. A. Baker and G. W. Tagg, located at 407 North Main Street in 1907. They "covered bicycles, automobiles, and all other kids of repairs," according to an advertisement in the *Polk City Directory* for Ellensburg. The shop changed ownership and later moved south on Main Street to the Arcade Building.

A group of motorcyclists pose in the snow on Main Street between Third and Fourth Avenues in 1916. The O. B. Castle Building, built in 1890, is behind the men on the far right, and Sam Pearson's building is on the left. The only identified men are Nick Daviscourt, fourth from the left, and Lee Scott is third from the right.

A group of motorcyclists are pictured on the east side of Main Street in front of the Arcade Building around 1916. The building was home to the Ellensburg Cycle Company, owned by R. W. Shepherd, and the Arcade Saloon, a popular and stylish establishment opened in 1908 by John H. Wippel. The Thor Motorcycle was in early contention with Harley Davidson and Indian but went out of business by 1920.

Nick Daviscourt shows off his Thor motorcycle, which he purchased at the Ellensburg Cycle Company on Main Street. Daviscourt was prominent in high school athletics in Ellensburg and began professional wrestling in local competitions around the Northwest. Daviscourt gained fame as a wrestler when he opposed Ed "Strangler" Lewis in New York City for the world championship in 1922. He did not win, but he continued to wrestle well into the 1920s.

The Chicago, Milwaukee, and Saint Paul Railroad decided to run a line through Ellensburg to compete with the Northern Pacific already established there. The railroad began work, buying land and laying tracks in 1906, and the first train arrived from Seattle in April 1909. This view is from Craig's Hill looking west back toward town.

The Chicago, Milwaukee, and Saint Paul depot in Ellensburg, which was located on Fourteenth Street in the empty lot that is now bordered by Water Street, Fourteenth Avenue, and the Mercer Creek Church. From this station, passengers could travel straight to Seattle over the Snoqualmie Pass, which was quicker than taking the Northern Pacific from Ellensburg to Tacoma via Stampede Pass, then north to Seattle.

The Northern Pacific Railway depot, built around 1886 when the train first came to Ellensburg, is seen here at the end of West Third Avenue. In the foreground is the staff from the Lunch Room, which sat just south of the depot and catered to hungry travelers. This depot was moved south in 1910 to make room for a brand new one and was used for storage. The Lunch Room was also closed, and food services were moved into the new depot.

120

The new Northern Pacific Railway depot in Ellensburg was built by contractor John Halloran of Lewiston, Idaho. Ellensburg was a popular stop on the Northern Pacific line, and the 1886 depot was showing signs of wear. Northern Pacific executives decided that Ellensburg needed a new depot as well as some additions to its roundhouse. Work began in 1909 on the roundhouse and new depot, and it officially opened in November 1910 to the excitement of the Ellensburg citizens. The massive structure offered steam heat, electric lights, lavatories, a ladies' private waiting room, a men's smoking room, and an area to rest or get something to eat. The roundhouse was torn down in the 1950s after a fire destroyed much of it. The depot was closed to train passengers in 1983 but still stands today.

Schoolteacher Florence Fischer is out for a frosty drive in 1916. The weather was so cold she not only bundled herself up, but put a blanket on the car's engine compartment as well. Florence's husband, Ray Fischer, was a bookkeeper, and both were active in the community. Their home was located at 808 East Sixth Avenue, across from Memorial Pool on Sixth Avenue today.

A group of men and boys gather around R. J. Alley's early Ford car on an Ellensburg street. Standing just to the left of the center pole is Alley, the owner of the Alley Transfer and Storage Company. Alley came to Ellensburg in 1901 and worked for various farmers until 1910, the year he started his business. He operated his business until he retired in the 1950s.

Eight
TOWN SCENES

This view looks south on Pearl Street across the intersection of Fifth Avenue and Pearl Street in 1915. On the right was Reynolds Garage, operated by Alfred Reynolds, which now serves as Sears. Across Fifth Avenue on the left sits the Ellensburg National Bank, which was built before the fire of 1889 and escaped the flames. Down the street on the left are the cupolas of the Davidson and Kreidel Buildings.

Deep snow filled the streets and was piled high on the sidewalks during the winter of 1916 in Ellensburg. Looking north on Pearl Street at the intersection of Pearl and Fourth Avenue, the large Cadwell-Olympic Building sits on the corner, followed by the Lynch Building, the Farmer's Bank Building, and the Antler's Hotel. The Lynch Building was constructed before the fire of 1889 and still stands today.

The Ellensburg National Bank Building, identified on page 123, was remodeled and reopened in 1930 as the National Bank of Ellensburg. In 1937, the bank went out of business, and the building was sold to the City of Ellensburg at auction for $10,000. The city's municipal offices were moved into the building in February 1938 and remained there until moving to their current home in 2004.

The Greyhound bus station sat on the southwest corner of Fifth Avenue and Pine Street. Greyhound operated out of this location until 1958, when it moved into the Antler's Hotel. After the bus station, a J. C. Penney's store moved into this corner after an extensive renovation. Penney's lasted nearly 40 years in this spot before closing its doors. The location is currently a Dollar Tree bargain store.

North Pearl Street between Eighth and Sixth Avenues was commonly referred to as "the Heights" due to the natural raise in elevation. The beautiful, large George E. Dickson home on the right was one of the architectural gems of this residential area. In-town irrigation, cement sidewalks, and streetlights revealed Ellensburg's modern and progressive nature during the first quarter of the 20th century.

The Cadwell Building, on the southwest corner of Third Avenue and Pine Street, is shown here as it appeared in the 1950s. Hughes Pontiac sold new and used cars, and the ground floor of the building was converted into a showroom. Thankfully this facade was removed, and the original Cadwell Building was revealed once again. The Kittitas County Historical Museum purchased the museum in 1974 and resides there today.

The Honolulu Block, located on the northeast corner of Pearl Street and Fifth Avenue, was built in 1889 by the McCandless brothers, who had large land and water investments in Honolulu, Hawaii Territory. Swangler's Furniture and Appliance was the occupant in this early-1960s view. This building was torn down in April 1966 to build a new Bank of Commerce building, which is a U.S. Bank today.

BIBLIOGRAPHY

An *Illustrated History of Klickitat, Yakima and Kittitas Counties, with an Outline of the Early History of the State of Washington*. Chicago, IL: Interstate Publishing Company, 1904.

Eberhart, Cory J. *The Building of Ellensburg*. Ellensburg, WA: Eberhart, 1976.

Fleming, Edna M. *Ah Kittitas!* Yakima, WA: Franklin Press, 1969.

Glauert, Earl T., and Merle H. Kunze. *Kittitas Frontiersmen*. Ellensburg, WA: Ellensburg Public Library, 1976.

———. *Kititas Indians*. Ellensburg, WA: Ellensburg Public Library, 1972.

Kittitas County Centennial Committee. *A History of Kittitas County, Washington, 1989*. Ellensburg, WA: The Committee, 1989.

Ludtka, John. *The Tradition Lives: a 75 Year History of the Ellensburg Rodeo*. Ellensburg, WA: Ellensburg Rodeo Association, 1997.

Owen, Barb. *Making the Grade: Plucky Schoolmarms of Kittitas Country*. Pullman, WA: Washington State University Press, 2008.

Splawn, A. J. *Ka-Mi-Akin, Last Hero of the Yakimas*. Caldwell, ID: Caxton Printers, Ltd., 1958.

Visit us at
arcadiapublishing.com